Achieve a Life of Wellness

The Road Map to Regaining
and Maintaining Your Health
Independence for Life

ACHIEVE A LIFE OF WELLNESS

The Road Map to Regaining and Maintaining Your Health Independence for Life

Jimmy Yen, LAc

YouSpeakIt
PUBLISHING
The Easy Way to Get Your Book Done Right™

Copyright © 2019 Jimmy Yen, LAc

All rights reserved. No part of this book may be reproduced or transmitted in any form or by any means without written permission of the publisher, except in the case of brief quotations embodied in critical articles and reviews.

This material has been written and published solely for educational purposes. The author and the publisher shall have neither liability nor responsibility to any person or entity with respect to any loss, damage, or injury caused or alleged to be caused directly or indirectly by the information contained in this book.

The author of this book does not dispense medical advice or prescribe the use of any technique as a form of treatment for physical, emotional, or medical problems without the advice of a physician, either directly or indirectly. The intent of the author is only to offer information of a general nature to help the reader in the quest for well-being. In the event the reader uses any of the information in this book for self or others, which is a constitutional right, the author and the publisher assume no responsibility for the actions of the reader.

Statements made in this book have not been evaluated by the Food and Drug Administration. This book and its contents are not intended to diagnose, treat, or cure any infection, injury, or illness, or prevent any disease. Results vary and each person's experience is unique.

Statements made and opinions expressed in this publication are those of the author and do not necessarily reflect the views of the publisher or indicate an endorsement by the publisher.

ISBN: 978-1-945446-45-0

First, I would like to dedicate this book to my wife, Jessica, for being my all-inclusive support team, and a special shout out to Brenda Lewis.

Second, I would like to dedicate this book to the millions of health sufferers who have been to all the specialists, both conventional and holistic, and still are not living the quality of life that they so desire.

Third, I would like to dedicate this book to all the healthcare practitioners who are reading this because they want to better serve their patients.

Contents

Acknowledgments	9
Introduction	11

CHAPTER ONE
Mindset	21
Deciding To Change	21
Breaking Old Habits	28
Continuing To Move Forward	32

CHAPTER TWO
Detox And Nutrition	41
Removing Interference	41
Supplying What's Missing	50
The Protocol	58

CHAPTER THREE
Fitness	69
Fitness Demystified	69
Aerobic Fitness	74
Anaerobic Fitness	81

CHAPTER FOUR
Hormones And Organ Function	89
Who Does The Healing?	89
Are Your Organs Communicating?	95
Have You Had The Proper Testing?	101

CHAPTER FIVE
   Nervous System   111
      Who Is The Master Of Your Body?   111
      Is There Something Wrong With Your Circuitry?   116
      How To Reconnect The Circuitry In Your Body   121

Conclusion   129
Next Steps   133
About the Author   135

Acknowledgments

There are so many people who have played a vital role in the writing of this book and the founding of this new movement called *Functional Wellness,* and they have been a great source of support, inspiration, and kick-in-the-butt motivation. I am sure I will fail to mention some in this section, so I apologize in advance.

First and foremost, I would like to thank my wife, who is my core and the only person who has truly been through thick and thin with me. Without her, there is no me, period.

Next, I would like to thank my parents, as they were the ones who passed down to me the tradition and knowledge of healthy living. Even though our relationship has been rocky, because they lead by example, their habits are infused into me. There's no better way of teaching than to walk your talk, and my parents are the epitome of that.

A special thanks to my clinical mentors and coaches; I definitely would not have been able to achieve a 90 percent success rate without their help: the late Richard Tan, for teaching me how to provide instant pain relief with acupuncture; Dr. Jimmy Chang, for teaching me how to interpret pulse findings to help patients identify which organs are malfunctioning; Dr. Gui-Li Zheng and Dr. Jimmy Chang, for teaching me how to produce phenomenal results using Chinese herbal medicine; and my dad, Jim Yen, for imparting me with the knowledge of nutrition and how to use food to heal the body.

Without all these people, I wouldn't have the knowledge, success, and expertise to write this book. I am truly humbled by their generosity.

Introduction

This book is a road map for your health journey. I like to call it the *road map to your health independence.* And the first step is to figure out which direction to go in.

For example, if you have an underactive thyroid, that doesn't mean you should take the same path as everyone else who has an underactive thyroid. A medical diagnosis is just a label; it doesn't tell you the root cause of your health issue.

This book is not like every other book on the market. It is not based on general theories, but on time-tested knowledge. It provides a detailed map that will get you started and show you the shortest distance you need to travel to reach health independence for the rest of your life.

My purpose is to help as many people as possible regain and maintain their body's natural ability to heal, so that they can live a happy and high-quality life. That is what life is all about. Unfortunately, we have been brainwashed by so much misinformation in the media, and there has not been a book available that has presented a demonstrable, proven system.

I want to share this knowledge and a tried-and-true program that produces results. To help you achieve your health independence, you'll need empowerment and correct information. These are the beginning steps that will give you insight into how to take control of your health. I'm not going to sugarcoat it for you: this is not a short-term solution; this is for the long term. And this is just the first book and road map, to get you started. Future books, or road maps, will be written to help you continue on your health journey.

Of course, there are many health books already, but most of them deliver only short-term solutions. Even though they may provide natural solutions, they are still not time-tested. The information in this book has provided results for three thousand years. If that is not enough evidence, I don't know what is. Many other nutrition and health books are based on recent information or recent research, which can change from year to year.

Ten years ago, we were advised that eating an egg was terrible, but now, it is the best thing. Three thousand years ago, people knew that eggs were a great source of nutrition for optimal health, but as time passed, businesses with private interests tried to prove that eggs were harmful to the human body. This thought was prevalent back in the days when the media promoted low fat diets. The food industry was manipulating research data to encourage the public to buy certain foods.

Ten years later, new research now says eggs are a superfood that benefit the human body and do not raise cholesterol.

This is just another example of how we cannot always rely on the current research because research on nutrition changes year to year.

Three thousand years ago, they knew that eating an egg was a good thing, but people did all this research to prove it wrong. Then they learned that their research was incorrect. It is a vicious cycle.

Here's another example. In September 2016, the *New York Times* came out with an article from a whistleblower who revealed the truth about the sugar industry. In the 1960s, the sugar industry paid Harvard scientists to manipulate research to show that fat was the cause of heart disease—not sugar. This was the main reason we were told to stay away from eating fat in the 1960s.[1]

We all started eating carbohydrates and guess what happened?

Diabetes became an epidemic, which it continues to be. This was all due to the food industry manipulating the so-called research. We now know that sugar is the cause of heart disease and many other chronic diseases.

---

[1] nytimes.com/2016/09/13/well/eat/how-the-sugar-industry-shifted-blame-to-fat.html?_r=0

In that same *New York Times* article, it reported that the *New England Journal of Medicine* did not require financial disclosures until 1984. That meant that all the research published in the *New England Journal of Medicine* could be bought, paid for, and manipulated by the pharmaceutical, agriculture, and food industries, and anybody else who had money. The *New England Journal of Medicine* is the main journal educating physicians about recent medical information from which they develop your treatment protocols.

My point is to be wary of anyone saying, "Based on the latest research, you should take this medication or take this supplement, or avoid eating this food."

Bottom line: you need to research the research. Find out who paid for the research and who's benefitting from the research. Don't just blindly believe.

Many medical schools and medical research firms are now funded by Big Pharma, and guess what they want those physicians to be doing when they treat you?

I encourage you to have a skeptical mind when seeking information to improve your health.

If we can't trust the latest research, what can we do?

Most of the new research has not withstood the test of time, as seen with the sugar industry in the 1960s.

Questions you should always ask are:

- Has the solution I'm being presented with been tested over time?
- What was the size of the study?

I can tell you that the solutions in this book have not changed for three thousand years, and they have been tested on millions of people.

Since this book is a road map, I want you first to read it quickly. Enjoy it the first time. Don't take any notes. Relax, and enjoy the book. Let it pique your mind and think about questions that may pop up.

Then I want you to read it again. The second time, I want you to start taking notes and writing down questions as you go through the details. The first time, it may take you a day to read it. The second time, it may take you a week. I want you to grab a notepad to write on and take some notes because this is a personal experience. Every time I read a book, I find something new that I missed before. It does not matter how thick or thin the book is; there are always gems. I want you to take your time during your second reading and write down all those questions and notes.

Try to get an overall picture of your health. Practice what it is to see the forest, rather than not see the forest for the trees. I will focus future books on the individual trees, but I want you to understand the overall concept of how to regain your health independence. You will see that the ideas are so simple. It may be difficult to do, but health in general is simple. We like to complicate things with technology, new information, and misleading research. Focus on the big picture as you read this book.

What I hope you get out of this book is the overall picture, understanding what I call the five stepping-stones to health independence:

- Mindset
- Detox and nutrition
- Fitness
- Hormones and organ function
- Nervous system

Understand that your mindset is key. It dictates everything, both physically and emotionally; emotionally, in that if you don't take care of your mind and emotions, everything you do for your physical health won't matter too much. You must understand what the priority is in your life: mindset.

I hear a lot of people say they want to achieve health, but when I ask them to change their diet, lifestyle, or to invest in their health, they are less interested. They then spend their money and time on vacations, houses, and cars. You can see where their priorities are by how they live their lives. This saddens me. The fact that you have picked up this book means you know something is wrong and you want and need to do something about it. You don't want to wait until you can't walk anymore, are sitting in a wheelchair on a feeding tube, or have lost the ability to care for yourself.

Right?

I want you to gain the road map for your health from this book. After reading it, you should be able to come up with a starting point and a continuing action plan. When you do any type of project, you don't just dive into it. You plan it from beginning to end, and when you do that, you work more efficiently and don't become distracted. This book will guide you to be efficient and effective with the decisions you make regarding your health.

I want you to enjoy it. You want to enjoy your health, and I want you to enjoy this book. Enjoy, and if you have any questions, look forward to my future books. You can find more information by visiting my website, AchieveIntegrativeHealth.com.

But for now, just enjoy. Sit back and relax.

CHAPTER ONE

Mindset

DECIDING TO CHANGE

To make a permanent change in any part of your life — whether regarding your health, your family life, or your personal finances — you must decide to want to change. Your mindset is the most important ingredient in you regaining your health independence.

What Do You Want?

When deciding to change, you must have an idea of what you want. You need to have the end goal in sight. If you are driving a car and don't have a destination, then you are driving all over, not knowing where you're going. In life and in health, it's the same.

You need to have a goal that is written down, in black and white, so you know what you are reaching for. Regarding health, for example, if you have diabetes, you probably want to reverse that condition. If you are on medications, you may not want to be dependent on them for the rest of your life. Maybe your goal is to have health independence, where you control your health by yourself and other health practitioners are merely alongside to assist you.

What's a good example of a goal?

A financial goal could be financial freedom. One goal could be to spend more time with your family. But your health is the foundation that gives you the ability to reach all your other goals.

Health affects every aspect of your life; without it, can you really be as productive or enjoy your life as much?

How long will you have that new purse, new car, or new house, and how long will you have your body?

We need to do more than give lip service to our health. If you say your health is the most important thing, then do something about it. Too often, when people ask me what they can do to regain their health independence, and I give them the solution, their responses shock me.

Some patients ask if insurance covers the program. Medical insurance was not created to help you regain your health independence.

And what if medical insurance doesn't cover the services you need to regain your health?

Does that mean you are going to let your health continue to deteriorate, just because insurance doesn't cover it?

We all know we need to eat healthy food to improve our health.

Well, does insurance cover your food? It doesn't, right?

Does that mean you're going to stop eating food because your insurance doesn't cover it?

Other patients tell me it's too expensive to be healthy.

What's the point of living in a new house and driving a new car if you are too sick to enjoy them?

What's the point of going to Paris for a vacation if you feel like crap the whole time?

And while you have all these new shiny things, your health is deteriorating and eventually you will need to have surgery to replace parts and remove organs because the damage is so bad, it's irreversible.

Is spending a few thousand dollars to restore your organ function more expensive than having to spend hundreds of thousands of dollars on surgery and medications because you chose not to invest in restoring your health initially?

Why Do You Want What You Want?

Once you determine what you want, you may find that you have many goals; however, you need to prioritize them. Let's use the driving analogy again to show the importance of prioritizing your goals. Let's say you want to go to Dallas, Austin, and San Antonio. If you haven't prioritized the order in which you want to visit these cities, then you are just blindly driving, lost, without knowing where to go.

You should determine what is most important, what each goal means to you, and how important each one is to you. If you don't achieve your health goals, you can't achieve any other goals. I can't tell you that health is your goal; you must determine that yourself. You need to identify your most important goals.

If finances, money, and time were not issues — think about this — what would you want to do?

How would you want to spend your days?

What would you be doing now?

The answer will steer you in the direction of your priority. This is not an easy task. But once you identify it, things fall into place and progress very smoothly.

Are You Insane?

A clever person once said, "If you continue to do the same thing and expect a different result, then, by definition, you are insane."

Are you insane?

Are you doing the same things over and over and expecting different results?

If you are, then you are like a hamster running on a wheel forever, but going nowhere. If you don't want that, if you feel like that, then it is time to change. You need to do something different. Remember, if you do the same thing over and over, you are going to get the same results. If you want a different result, you need to change it up.

You need to do something different. At the very least, it will get your foot off that hamster wheel. As you move off that wheel, you will notice that your opportunities are endless. You must set the intention in your mind to step off the hamster wheel, so that you can be open to your options. You need to try something different.

When my dad was in his twenties and thirties, he had developed some sinus issues, allergies, and immune system problems. Like many people, he went to the pharmacy and bought some over-the-counter medications, which helped. Over time, the medications stopped working. He next increased his medications, which helped, but a few months later, they stopped working again. He called his family doctor.

Guess what the doctor gave him?

Stronger medications. Prescription medications. They initially worked phenomenally, taking away all his symptoms: no fatigue, no headaches, no sinus problems. In the next couple years, things started creeping up again. Eventually, all his symptoms returned. So, he called his physician again.

Guess what his physician told him?

"Increase the dosage; let's also try some new medications."

Again, it worked . . . for a few years. Then, lo and behold, the symptoms came back. Since he had tried every single medication possible, his doctor sent him to an ear, nose, and throat specialist (ENT), who did a CT scan of his head and sinuses and found that there was an abnormal growth in his sinuses. The ENT wanted to do surgery, of course, so my dad went into surgery. They took out the growth, and he felt great for a couple years.

Then his symptoms started to creep back slowly. He ran through the same routine again: over-the-counter medications, prescription medications, back to the ENT, CT scan, and they found that the growth had come back. Of course, the ENT wanted to do surgery again, so my dad had a second surgery. It was at that time that he realized that over the past ten years, he had been doing the same thing and getting the same results. It was time to change.

What he mentally decided was: *I want a different result. That means I need to do something different.*

That is when he started to look for other ways to improve his health. On April 1, 2016, he celebrated his seventy-fifth birthday. He has not had another surgery since his thirties, nor taken any medications. He feels better than ever. A few years ago, he hiked the Mongolian mountains twice with twenty- and thirty-year-olds.

He is a prime example of someone who acted on the idea: *If you are not satisfied with the result that you are getting, you need to do something different.*

The reason we are spending a whole chapter on mindset is that change starts in your brain, in your mind. If you don't change your mindset, people can give you the secret sauces, the magic solutions, the keys to happiness, but none of it will work. You must change your mindset.

Don't take this chapter lightly. Really focus on answering the questions presented. Take some time to think about them. Don't breeze through. Take your time. Talk it over with your family. Really think through *why* you want to change.

BREAKING OLD HABITS

One of the topics we hear about most frequently about from patients in our clinic is bad habits; people have had habits for twenty to forty years, and either they don't think they can break them, or they are terrified of failing. Habits aren't created overnight—they are created over time. Therefore, in order to break habits, you must allow yourself the adequate time to address them.

Old habits may not be a bad thing. Most people may think old habits are bad, and we need to break them, but that is not necessarily the truth. We need to look at why you have these habits. If you understand that and how they are detrimental to your health, then it will be easier for you to relinquish them.

Can Anyone Do It?

The question many people ask when they come to our clinic is: *Can anyone do it?*

The answer is yes; anyone can break an old habit. It goes back to the previous section about deciding to change. Once you decide what you want, and you realize your habits are not helping you achieve what you want, it becomes easier. Remember, breaking a habit does not happen overnight. It requires work.

There are exercises to help you break bad habits. For example, if you drink coffee all the time, there may be a reason you are addicted to coffee. Maybe you need coffee for energy.

What if you solved the problem?

What if you addressed why you didn't have enough energy, why you were fatigued?

Then, you wouldn't need the coffee. Automatically, it would be easy for you to give up coffee. I am not saying everybody should give up coffee. This is just an example. If we can identify why you have certain habits, find the cause, and address the cause, then we can help you break those habits. It is the same process when it comes to reversing any chronic, degenerative health disorder.

Don't Focus on Getting Rid of Habits

The focus on these habits should not be: *Okay, what do I need to get rid of? I should get rid of bread, sugar, coffee, and chocolate.*

If you think in that direction, then making changes will be difficult because you are thinking about what you are giving up; your focus is on deprivation. For some of you, these are pleasure items. To be healthy and gain health independence does not mean you must give up all these things. No one lives in a bubble, and we all have certain enjoyments. When those enjoyments become detrimental to your health on a daily basis, they become a problem. Again, we want to focus on why you have these habits in the first place.

How did they develop in the beginning?

It may have been in childhood or in adulthood. If we can figure out why you developed that habit, we can look for solutions to address the cause, and naturally you will modify those habits.

The Reward of Freedom

One of the best ways to break old habits is to focus on the reward or the goal that you will achieve by eliminating them from your life. In the previous section, we were looking at what you want. That is why I want you to take some time to focus on what you want, because if your desire is powerful enough, you will be willing to do anything and everything to get it.

For example, when you were younger, you may have wanted a particular house or car. It motivated you to act to achieve those goals: *I wanted this girl; I wanted this boy; I wanted to marry this person.* You just made it happen. You automatically disregarded any obstacles in your way. You were intent on your goal and would do whatever you needed to achieve it.

The key is to focus on your goal and your freedom.

When I say *freedom,* I mean:

- Health freedom
- Financial freedom
- Spiritual freedom

It does not matter; it all depends on what you want. Focus on the goal and keep the end in sight. That must be your purpose. If you do, then you will connect the dots.

Back to the driving analogy: if your goal is to find the shortest distance to Austin, you're not going to detour through Dallas or Houston or San Antonio. You're going to find the most direct route.

It's the same thing with your health goals. When you focus on your goal, certain habits that don't support that goal just drop off along the way naturally.

To summarize: to achieve your goal, you are not focusing on how to get rid of old habits, but rather, how to develop new habits. When you spend most of your time and energy on developing new habits, the old habits go away naturally.

However, some of those old habits may be good, and you may need to improve upon them. For example, some people have a habit of exercising every day, which may or may not be good for you. We will go into more detail about that later. Let's not focus on breaking any of our old bad habits, but instead, let's focus on creating new great habits.

CONTINUING TO MOVE FORWARD

No matter what you do in life to improve your health, your finances, your family, or your spirituality, you need to continue to move forward. Moving forward is the key to success. If you talk to any successful entrepreneurs or health coaches, they will tell you that what they have done is continue to move forward. Moving forward will be our focus for this section.

Peaks and Valleys

Now, you have decided to get off the hamster wheel, and you are going into unknown territory. You may be a little afraid, because nobody likes to fail. We all want to succeed with our first steps. But for most us, that does not happen. I know there are some people who try one thing, one time, and succeed on their first effort. That does not happen all the time, so, don't beat yourself up when it doesn't happen for you.

On your health journey, you will experience some peaks and valleys. The path to your goal will always be fluctuating; the key is to keep those peaks and valleys fluctuating only minimally. If you continue to move forward to reach your goals, then you will succeed in regaining your health independence.

Everybody — including myself — goes through peaks and valleys every day. That is why we have mentors who help pick us up if we fall off our program. Mentors and coaches play a crucial role. We all go through lapses. Who succeeds and who does not is a simple matter of who continues to move forward.

Don't be deterred by the valleys you go through. Learn from those, as they are the best times for learning. When things are rolling smoothly, you don't learn as much because you are not challenged. Take advantage of those valleys. It may not feel great when you are going through them, but if you change your mindset and continue to focus on what lesson you are supposed to learn from the valleys, your peaks will be even higher. Enjoy the peaks while you have them, and learn from the valleys when you are in them.

Every Master Was Once a Disaster

This is a famous quote used by many motivational speakers, health coaches, and entrepreneurs, and it is so true: "Every master was once a disaster."

Every master failed. In fact, they have failed more times than the average person. It's because of those failures that they are able to succeed and enjoy the big successes that they have had in life and in health.

This includes making changes in your lifestyle; you may not succeed all at once. Olympic athletes fail quite a bit, but they fail fast. You want to fail fast. That is the key. Olympic athletes fail fast, but they try again quickly until they master their sport.

That is what you need to do in your daily life. If you fall off the wagon, that's okay. Sure, you're not supposed to be having a doughnut. That is all right. You have a doughnut, and the next day, you start all over again. If you can start over every day, you will be on the right path.

If you work with mentors or coaches who have already made these mistakes themselves, their guidance can help you make fewer mistakes and reach your goal faster than you had anticipated. Let me emphasize: the role of mentor or coach is probably one of the most important roles to include in your support team. If you don't have one, you need to find one. I personally have six, and that is still not enough. I highly recommend mentors and coaches.

Life Is a Marathon, Not a Sprint

Many of you have probably heard this quote before: "Life is a marathon and not a sprint."

This is true regarding every aspect of your life, especially your health. There are so many fad diets available for people who want to lose weight. Most of these diets can help you lose weight, but the problem is they don't help you keep the weight off. Those diets are like a sprint. After you are done with a sprint, you are done.

Life is not like that. It's not like you go on the fad diet, lose the weight, and are done, and you can go back to your old daily habits. No, it does not work that way. Health and life are marathons; they are never-ending quests to keep yourself on track. If you treat it that way, if you view your health that way, you will continue to improve your health.

Every day, every one of us must work on our health. That is a fact that cannot be changed. The sooner we accept and realize it, the happier we are going to be. It's not about who gets healthier quicker. It's about developing permanent habits and permanent skills, which lead to permanent results. If that is what you want, you should treat this journey you are about to embark on as a marathon.

Do not be discouraged by people who lose weight faster than you or get off their medications faster than you. That is okay. Their bodies and your body are completely different. You need to focus on you.

You need to focus on your end goals:

- Health independence
- Organs that function at optimal capacity
- No medications
- Control over your health

These should be your focus. You are about to embark on a journey, a marathon journey.

To summarize: everything starts in your brain or your mind. How and what you think dictate how your body is going to respond. Know that whatever you think of yourself, you are always going to be *right* because your body is going to position itself to make your thoughts come true. If you think you can't reverse your diabetes, then your body is going to prove you right. However, if you think you can get pregnant, your body is also going to prove you right. Your emotions will always put your body in motion.

No matter what stage of health you are in, the key thing that my mentors consistently tell me is to continue to move forward. Put one foot in front of the other and do not stop. We human beings are good at procrastinating.

The moment you procrastinate, progress stops. But that's not the worst part: not only does progress stop, it reverses.

No matter what peaks and valleys or disasters you go through, you must continue to put one foot in front of the other and move forward.

One of my mentors told me, "You are going to make more right decisions than wrong decisions."

Think about that over the span of your whole life. Of all the decisions you have ever made, you most likely have made more great ones than bad ones. Don't be afraid to screw up. Don't be afraid to fall off the wagon. Continue to make decisions and continue to move forward.

CHAPTER TWO

Detox and Nutrition

REMOVING INTERFERENCE

In Chapter One, we addressed a key component to success on your journey to health independence: mindset. You must adopt the right mindset; otherwise, even if you are given the right tools, you won't be able to implement them and you won't succeed.

This chapter discusses some of the reasons for and some of the tools needed to gain health independence.

Let's use an analogy of a wilting plant. What do you need to do to revive it?

You need to provide it with nutrients, sunlight, and water. Let's say the soil was contaminated; perhaps someone put chemical fertilizer or motor oil in it. You would need to transplant the plant to more fertile soil and remove the toxins.

You can view your health in the same way you view the plant's health.

You need to do two things:

- Remove what is interfering
- Supply what's missing.

That is what we are going to talk about in this chapter.

The main cause of most health problems is stress.

When we use the term *stress,* we are referring to three types of stress:

- Physical
- Chemical
- Emotional

Physical Stress

An example of physical stress is being in a car accident, and your leg has been almost completely severed. It is barely attached to your body. You've got physical stress.

You may think that all athletes look very healthy, but actually many of them are not, because they put too much physical stress on their bodies. Athletes who run marathons or triathlons are a good example of this. If you have friends who do either, talk to them about their joints. In our clinic, we find that 90 percent of our athlete patients will wear down their joints faster than normal and develop arthritis.

One of the most common causes of death for marathon runners is heart attack. Marathon competitors push their bodies beyond their normal limits, which may seem glorious when they're holding up a trophy or making it into the record books, but they are accelerating the aging process. Now, I'm not advising you to never run a marathon; I'm just suggesting you limit yourself to one marathon a year.

While too much physical stress can have a negative effect on your body, so too can not *enough* physical stress. Physical stress is one of the causes we identify as interfering with your healing process. In Western medicine, we have imaging tools like CT scans and MRIs, which can be helpful in identifying any permanent damage from physical stress. In this situation, Western medicine is good; we need to combine it with natural holistic medicine.

Developing arthritis and scar tissue in your joints is not normal. Yes, it is very common. But just because something is common doesn't make it normal. Often the cause of arthritis and scar tissue is physical stress.

Chemical Stress

The second type of stress is chemical stress: for example, pollution.

Everything you put in your body creates either good or bad chemical stress. That is why diet is so important. If you have been eating junk food all your life, you have subjected your body to a lot of chemical stress. Over time, that chemical stress builds up and causes chronic degenerative disorders and super-accelerates the aging process.

Yes, you age much faster by eating the wrong diet that offers poor nutrition. So, if you want to continue to accelerate your aging process, continue to eat whatever unhealthy food you may currently be eating.

Environment is also a culprit of chemical stress. When Beijing, China, hosted the 2008 Olympics, no vehicles were permitted to be driven into the city and all factories were shut down in an effort to reduce pollution. The authorities noticed that the constant haze disappeared. They also noticed that the number of heart and lung diseases decreased. After the Olympics, all the factories opened again and cars went back into the city, and the pollution returned. Then, they noted that the cases of heart and lung diseases went back up.[2]

Environmental toxins, fertilizers, and genetically modified food all create chemical stress in your body, and it is slowly killing you, every day. Some of you may

---

2 cbsnews.com/news/reducing-air-pollution-during-2008-beijing-olympics-boosted-residents-heart-health-research-reveals/

already be experiencing symptoms caused by chemical stress, and some of you may not see symptoms for ten or twenty years down the road.

Just because you don't feel any of the damage yet doesn't mean your body is not deteriorating at a rapid pace. We've all known someone who went in for an annual checkup and was given a clean bill of health, only to drop dead the next day of a heart attack. Unfortunately, the first symptom—a problem with their heart—was also the last symptom they felt. Don't wait for symptoms to show up before you get serious about your health independence.

I've worked with many people who take one or two medications, yet tell me they are healthy, because with their medications they experience no symptoms. If you are taking even just one medication, you are not healthy. You are relying on a foreign substance to maintain your organ function. My definition of health is that the body is able to heal itself by itself. When you rely upon medication or surgery to heal, you are not healthy. Medications are toxins to the body and don't belong in the body.

Let's think about this.

When was the last time you heard that someone had an Advil deficiency?

When your healthcare provider orders a blood test, what are they testing for?

Most likely, they are testing for calcium, potassium, and a vitamin B12 deficiency. They are testing for the nutrients your body needs to self-heal.

If your body needs medications to regulate your blood pressure or your blood sugar, why doesn't your provider run a blood test to see if you have a lisinopril or metformin deficiency, two of the most common causes of those conditions?

It is important to know what type of chemical you are putting in your body in the form of medication.

Is it helping your body regenerate and keeping your organs functioning better, or is it doing the opposite?

It can only do one of two things: help you or hurt you. There is no neutral.

Emotional Stress

Emotional stress is the third type of stress. This is the one most people think about when using the term *stress*.

Who has emotional stress?

If you think you don't, you are lying to yourself. Everybody has emotional stress.

When I conduct my health training classes and ask people that question, everybody in the crowd raises their hands. Stress is part of normal life. There are different types of emotional stress—the kind that releases endorphins, such as getting ready for vacation or getting married, is called *eustress*. Harmful emotional stress is called distress.

In general, we have the same types of emotional stresses: friends, family, relationships, work, finances.

Why do some people freak out with anxiety attacks and panic attacks, while others don't?

The key is in understanding what helps your body adapt to stress: your organ function. If your organs are functioning up to par, they are going to help your body adapt to emotional stress so you can remain calm when your kids are not behaving or your boss is yelling at you.

You can't change what causes emotional stress. You can't quit your job, necessarily.

What can you change?

What you can change is your organ function. Via diet, exercise, and lifestyle changes, you can help the organs that are responsible for helping you adapt to stress function at optimal levels. These organs are called your *stress organs,* your liver and adrenal glands.

You can also change your daily facial habits. In fact, this is a secret solution to depression, stress, and anxiety. It does not involve a pill, lotion, or magic potion, and it costs you nothing. Yup, it's free!

Here's the secret: in 2003, Dr. Eric Finzi, a cosmetic surgeon, treated several subjects suffering from moderate to severe depression with Botox (botulinum toxin), paralyzing the muscles in their brows that create expression of sadness, anger, and fear. He found that nine out of ten patients reported a complete remission of their depression.[3]

No, I'm not telling you to get Botox—this example shows you that the expression on your face dictates your emotion.

So, the free secret weapon is a simple smile. Anytime you feel stressed, down, or depressed, force yourself to smile and hold that smile until you start feeling better. It doesn't matter if your smile looks fake, you will notice that if you hold your smile long enough it is virtually impossible for you to stay angry, depressed, or stressed—*mic drop!*

Is it going to eliminate your response to stress?

---

3 Finze, Eric and Erika Wasserman. "Treatment of Depression with Botulinum Toxin A: A Case Series." American Society for Dermatologic Surgery, Inc. 2006.

No, we all have our ups and downs. When those fluctuations are small, your organs are going to be functioning well, which means you will be functioning well. You will feel great. That is the point of life.

We have addressed the three main types of stress that cause health disorders. The first part of addressing toxins includes removing the interference, and stress is interference.

Assess your level of *physical stress*. If you are constantly overstressing yourself physically by working out seven days a week, that is not good. You should tone that down, as too much exercise is not good. On the other hand, if you are not working out at all, you are also creating physical stress, you need to start exercising.

To eliminate *chemical stress,* stop putting junk and toxins in your body. If you put toxins in your body, those toxins go into your blood. Point blank: stop putting toxins into your body and surround yourself with a chemical-free environment.

To address *emotional stress:*

- Get your organs functioning optimally. Get your organs in shape so they can adapt to the emotional stress, because often you can't change that stress. Sometimes you can.

- Find better ways to adapt to emotional stress. You may be able to quit your job or school, but you can't get rid of your children. You have to adapt.

- Decrease systemic inflammation. It will help you remove interference from all these stressors.

- Meditate and get into the right mindset.

The mind is a power organ; it controls every action and reaction in your body. So, finding new ways to process negative information, such as meditation, could literally change your life.

SUPPLYING WHAT'S MISSING

Let's go back to the plant analogy used in the previous section.

Remember, if you want to revive a wilting plant, what do you do?

You need to supply what is missing: sunlight, water, and nutrients. The same is true for the human body. We must supply what is missing. After we have removed the interference, we need to supply what is missing.

What is actually missing from our bodies?

Are You Following the Latest Diet Trend?

Whether you are trying to lose weight, get more energy, sleep better, or improve your brain functioning — your memory, most likely — you probably have tried various diets.

Let's use weight loss as an example, because there are so many weight loss programs available, many of which actually help you lose weight. However, they don't help you keep the weight off. You probably have noticed that once you lose weight on a particular diet, the weight comes back right on when you stop the diet. The reason is that you are not supplying what is missing. You are not helping your organs function better. That is what healing is all about: getting your organs functioning optimally.

If these diets were really supplying the nutrients that were missing from your organs, then once you stopped that diet, your organs would be functioning better, not worse.

For example, there was a high-protein diet that helped people lose weight rapidly. However, these people were later found to have liver or kidney disease; their organs were worse off than when they started.

People think you need to lose weight to get healthy, but it's actually the opposite — you need to get healthy to lose weight. Whether you want to lose weight, sleep better, or get more energy, it is all about supplying the right nutrients to your specific organs.

Of course, you must diagnose or determine which organ is malfunctioning. That is key, because you can't randomly throw nutrients in your body and hope organ function improves. You need to be specific. Being specific means finding out which organs are malfunctioning and then finding the right process to reintroduce the needed nutrients to those organs to improve their ability to function. And then, even if you fall off the wagon once in a while, your body will have the ability to eliminate whatever toxins you put in your mouth.

If you are following the latest diet trends, then you are probably not addressing the root cause of the malfunction. Trends change. Every year, there is a new diet. Diets are all about helping you lose weight fast, without addressing the root cause. The root cause is what can help you improve organ function.

Quality Versus Quantity

Once you have determined which organs are the main ones that are dysfunctional, then you can figure out what nutrients and foods you need to consume. Everybody knows that organic food is good; however, if you just fill yourself with organic food, you may notice a small improvement, but you will not get the results you want.

Let's talk about organic food. Some people wonder if it really matters whether a food is organic. After all, it's still evident in organic foods that our soils are depleted of minerals, vitamins, and nutrients. However, if you ate conventional food, you would need to eat two or three times more to get the same nutrients as the organic equivalent. So, quality significantly matters. If you only have one choice, buy organic.

Organically grown food is not the only healthy choice. Your local vegetable farmers can grow healthy food even without the organic certification, but you need to talk to them and ask how they manage fertilizing soil, controlling pests, and whether they use GMOs. A good farmer takes care of the soil. When it's well tended in a sustainable way, local soil is your best bet for getting the nutrients you need to live in your geographic area.

Organic food is available to many of us both frozen and fresh: which is better?

Most people would think that fresh is better, but the answer is actually frozen.

Frozen organic fruits and vegetables are picked later in the season, so they are allowed to ripen before they are picked and frozen. The plant is allowed to grow to its fullest potential so you get the highest amount of nutrients. Most fresh, organic berries, for example, are imported from South America, so they are picked early to be shipped to the United States. They are picked before they are ripe, so they don't contain all the nutrients.

Can You Eat for Pleasure?

Many people are like me in the sense that they love to eat.

Some people are thinking: *Do I need to sacrifice my ability to eat for pleasure in order to get healthy?*

The answer is no. I love to eat every type of food. However, I know that some types of food are detrimental to the body, so I don't eat them every day.

How can I position myself so I can still enjoy eating, yet still be healthy?

Here is a secret. When people go through our wellness programs, I always give them a final goal. That way, they know what they are shooting for.

To the people who are like me and love to eat, I say, "This is the goal: five days out of the week, you eat healthy, strictly following the regimen. Then two days out of the week, you can cheat and eat whatever you want."

One of my mentors, Dr. Hiromi Shinya, author of *The Enzyme Factor*, states in his book that he would rather his patients eat a somewhat decent diet and be happy about it, than eat a perfect diet and be miserable.

Now, this is not a get-out-of-jail-free card. I'm not saying you can eat whatever you want. The point is that you need a balance of a healthy mindset and a healthy diet.

That is how I live my life right now. Five days out of the week, I am working on improving my health, improving the function of my organs and getting them strong. Come the weekend, I will be eating some not-so-healthy foods, but my organs are going to be so healthy that they can process and eliminate all those toxins and chemical stresses I will be enjoying.

This is something I like to tell my patients, so they have something to look forward to. And it does not mean you *must* cheat two days out of the week; some people don't like to cheat and prefer to eat nutritiously every day.

When you are eating healthy and your organs are functioning better, you start becoming sensitive to junk and toxins. When you eliminate all the toxins from your body and start eating better, and you attempt to put junk food back into your body, your body will reject it, and it will let you know.

When you go back to junk food, your body may experience symptoms, such as:

- Nausea
- Stomachaches
- Muscle cramps
- Diarrhea
- Constipation
- Fatigue
- Constant throat clearing

It will let you know that the junk food and toxins don't belong in your body, and it is your job to listen to your body.

Your body is a diagnostic machine. It is better than MRIs or ultrasounds. Nobody can tell you how you feel better than you can, so you must learn to listen to your body.

As you put junk into your body, it loses the ability to identify what is toxic and what is not. That is how people develop autoimmune diseases. If you want to reverse autoimmune disease, you need to recalibrate your immune system, your organ functioning, and your gut. Through our program, your body will be resensitized and recalibrated to identify what is normal and what is a toxin.

Regaining your health independence and organ function is simple:

1. You need to remove what is interfering with optimal organ function.
2. You need to find what is missing that is preventing your organs from functioning and supply it.

Otherwise, it does not matter how many nutrients you put in your body; they aren't going to work.

You must take both these steps to gain health independence. My goal is to help our patients and our community regain health independence so they are not dependent on medications and surgeries. I want them to be 100 percent in control of their own health.

When you are thinking about health—medical procedures, natural procedures, medications—always refer back to these two questions:

1. What is interfering?
2. What am I missing?

These two questions will guide you to the right solution.

THE PROTOCOL

Our clinic has a high success rate. The reason is because we have a system. Many people have tried so many different things to improve their health, like dieting and detoxing. But the results are either not easily maintained or do not last, and people may not get the results they want.

More importantly, most people do not achieve the success they want, and they sell themselves short. The reason they don't get the results they want is because they don't have a system. They are trying different approaches, and they'll never succeed that way. If I gave you the correct directions to get to our clinic, but I gave them to you in the wrong order, you are not going to get to our clinic. That is what you are doing when you keep trying the latest fad or trend. Trying this and that doesn't necessarily mean you will arrive at your destination.

In our clinic, we provide a step-by-step system. You must address health independence in a systematic way. As American engineer and management consultant W. Edwards Deming said, "Ninety-four percent of failure is the result of the system, not people." If you are tired of doing the same thing and getting the same result, you need to do something different to get a different result. If you do not use a systematic approach, you are not going to succeed.

Optimal health of the human body depends on the five main pillars of health:

1. Mindset
2. Detox and nutrition
3. Fitness
4. Hormones and organ function
5. Nervous system

Ask yourself: *Which one of these five pillars can I truly do without?*

That is the focus in subsequent chapters. We have already talked about detox and nutrition, but we go into more detail, so be ready to take lots of notes.

A System for Success

The reason we have a high success rate at our clinic is because we have a system. Going back to the five pillars, you must do certain things in a certain order. For example, some people have tried to improve their nutrition. But like I said, when you just pump yourself full of organic food without detoxing first, you won't get the best results, because you need to clean your house before you put new stuff inside.

If you don't clean the filters in your car, and you keep putting more gasoline in, those clogged filters eventually will prevent your car from running smoothly. The same is true for your body. You need to detox.

Detoxing is not about making you go to the restroom fifty times a day; it is different. You will learn the right way to detox.

Phase One: Detox

Step one of our system is detox.

What does *detox* actually mean?

Most people have gone online and searched for cleanses, but that is not what detoxing your system is about. You must understand that some organs naturally detox your body by themselves. The reason you are not full of toxins right now is because those organs are functioning at 100 percent. Detox focuses on organ function.

What organs are we looking at when it comes to detoxing naturally?

We focus on three organs when detoxing:

- Liver
- Gut
- Kidneys

If all three organs are functioning close to 100 percent, your body naturally detoxes. But if you are not feeling well and are experiencing unwanted symptoms, then these organs are not functioning. You can help them function better.

How do we do that?

We can do lab tests; this is where Western medicine excels. Certain lab tests can help us identify which organs are not functioning up to par. In traditional Chinese medicine, there is a diagnostic tool that we use called *functional pulse diagnosis* (FPD). FPD is the palpation of the radial artery to detect organ function. Three thousand years ago, people found that different sections of the radial artery correspond to different organ systems. Through palpating these different sections, the tester can feel blood being pumped to each organ in the body, providing information about how well the organs are functioning.

This can help determine which organs are not functioning well. Again, what is interfering needs to be removed from these organs, and what is missing needs to be supplied.

The liver, gut, and kidneys: is there anything interfering in their healing process?

If so, we need to remove it.

Is there anything missing?

If so, we need to supply it.

Our normal detox process is a four-week process. Detox does take some time, because it takes time to restore organ function. Any detox that takes one or two days really is not going to produce results. It is too shocking for the body. Detox should be a natural, slow process. We are trying to restore organ function, which is not something that can be done overnight.

Phase Two: Nutrition

After you have completed the four weeks of detox, we do a stool analysis because we want to make sure you successfully removed the toxins from your body.

We want to make sure there is no overgrowth of:

- Bacteria
- Fungus
- Yeast
- Parasites

We want to make sure your gut is clear. You normally have yeast and friendly bacteria in your body, but you don't want them to be overgrowing.

If the stool analysis comes back positive, then you did not clear everything, and you will need to do the detox again until it is cleaned up. Once you get a clear sample, you will have completed the detox successfully, and you can move on to the next phase, which focuses on nutrition.

Nutrition

We must put the right nutrition into your body. This is where organic or the best-sourced food comes in. There are specific foods that benefit specific organs. We need to identify which organs are malfunctioning and which are missing nutrition, so we can supply the right nutrition. For example, if you were having trouble with the liver, you'd want to make sure to eat lots of cruciferous vegetables—broccoli, kale, cauliflower, and brussels sprouts. They are liver-loving foods and cancer-fighting vegetables. If your kidneys, which are water organs, are having issues, you need to supply water-filled fruits—such as watermelon, cantaloupe, and honeydew—for their optimal functioning.

Putting the right nutrition into your body is vital. If you put the wrong nutrition in, it may not be harmful, but it won't give you the maximum results.

We want to achieve the maximum results in the least amount of time to be the most efficient. That is what we do in a system. When you are not using a system, you are not being efficient with your time, money, or eating. Instead of going from point A to B in a straight line, you are zigzagging everywhere. Most of us like the shortest route, and a system helps us get where we want to go in the shortest amount of time.

If I can stress it again: it is so important to have a system. Without a system, you won't get the results you want, and you are basically just going halfway. Remember, 94 percent of failure is the failure to have a system.

If you wanted to learn how to fly a plane, what would you need?

You would need:

- A manual
- A class
- A plane

Could you fly a plane by yourself just from reading a manual?

What about just from going to class?

Probably not. And even if you had a plane, that wouldn't mean you knew how to fly it.

What are you missing?

You are missing that teacher, instructor, mentor, or coach. That is what you also need.

Why is it any different for your health?

Have you ever invested in a system run by a mentor or coach?

If you haven't, that may be the reason you are not getting the results you want. In addition to the five pillars of health, you need a mentor or coach. That could be the missing piece on your journey to health independence.

My mom is one of seven kids. Her fourth-oldest brother was diagnosed with Parkinson's disease quite a few years ago. His wife is a believer in traditional Western medicine. She believes physicians are gods and that everything they say is scripture. If a physician told her that rat poison was good for her health, she would drink it up. So, they started my uncle on medications for Parkinson's, and he was getting worse over time. My mom, being more knowledgeable about natural medicine, would take a Vitamix blender to his house and blend fruits and vegetables. For three months, she would go to his house in Taiwan every day — they lived pretty close — and make the blended smoothie for him. In three months, the Parkinson's symptoms started to diminish. It was actually reversing. But my aunt, for some reason, could not change her mindset. She could not see the improvement.

She told my mom, "No, it's not working. Stop coming here."

Of course, my mom stopped going over. And, his Parkinson's got worse again. Now, it is to a point where he cannot even walk; he needs to be in a wheelchair. The Parkinson's is so severe that he is losing his bodily functions.

At what point do you start looking at results instead of something that has been scientifically proven with a double-blind study?

Much of the research done today is funded by pharmaceutical companies.

Take a guess. What do you think they want the research to prove?

The point is, when you supply the body with what it needs, miraculous things happen. When you put poison into your body — poison being medication — it will go in the opposite direction. My mom personally saw that happen to her brother, and unfortunately, we were not able to educate my aunt and convince her that all the medications were hurting her husband.

That experience showed me that simple things, such as supplying what is missing and removing the toxins, can change your health and your life. It may sound so simplistic, but health is that simple. We simply need to stop complicating things.

CHAPTER THREE

Fitness

FITNESS DEMYSTIFIED

Fitness is one of the five pillars of health. Everybody needs fitness. Fitness doesn't just affect your physical body, it also affects your mental and emotional well-being. One of my mentors told me, *motion becomes emotion.*

Basically, the human body was built to be in motion. As long as you are in motion, it is difficult for you to be stressed and depressed. When certain people hear *fitness,* they think about cardio, but others think about weights and resistance training. Whatever your definition, fitness is mandatory. There is so much fitness information out there, and every year something new comes out, like P90X or CrossFit.

Which ones are necessary, and which ones are good to use to restore your health?

They are all different. In this chapter, we are going to demystify what really works and what fitness activities may be hurting you.

Fitness Is Mandatory for Optimal Health

Fitness is one of the five pillars of health, which also includes:

- Mindset
- Detox and nutrition
- Hormones and organ function
- Nervous system

One thing I like to ask people is, "Which one of these can you do without?"

You can't do without any of them. For diabetics, for example, fitness is highly mandatory. If they do not exercise, they will not be able to lower their blood sugar or maintain good blood sugar levels. So, it is not a choice for them; it is mandatory.

Let's look at the two types of fitness. The most important muscle is your heart, and there is a certain type of fitness to strengthen your heart: cardio. Strength training works to strengthen the muscles that hold your spine and organs in place. Both types are mandatory to keep you at optimal health.

If your heart is not beating strongly, then you are not adequately pumping blood through your body, and your organs are not going to function correctly. The same thing is true with the muscles in the rest of your body. If your muscles are weak, then they are not supporting you. Of course, you will have pain, but parts may be moving in your spine that should not be moving. Movement in your spine could press on a nerve, which could prohibit different organs from working. But the root cause would have been not having strong enough muscles to support your back and spine. That is why exercise is mandatory, not optional.

Train Smarter, Not Harder

A common misconception about fitness is that you need to work out seven days a week, one hour every day. That is not correct; more is not better in this situation. People may do CrossFit or run five miles five days a week, but they are hurting themselves more than helping. When you see people who are fit with chiseled muscles, they are not necessarily healthier. Learn how to train correctly.

Especially for those of us who don't like exercising, why not be efficient?

To be most efficient and effective:

- Find the right type of exercise for you.
- Find out what intensity you need to do.
- Find out the correct duration of time for you.

If you can determine those details, you will be training smarter, not harder. If you want to exercise to gain optimal health, all you need is two to three times per week, thirty minutes each time, with a maximum of two hours per week. You can achieve optimal health that way.

How does that sound to you?

Is that doable?

Now, if you are bodybuilding, then it's a whole different story. Bodybuilding is not about health.

Is Your Fitness Hurting You?

Train smarter, not harder. Do not fall for the myth of needing to exercise seven days a week to be healthy and strong. Many of us overtrain. An example is someone whose organs are not functioning up to par. If their adrenal glands are weak, and they do intense interval trainings, they are actually going to make themself worse by making their adrenal glands even more fatigued. You may think your exercise is helping you, but in reality, it may be hurting you.

Exercising at the correct intensity for the right amount of time can make the difference between that exercise helping you or hurting you.

How can you tell what's right for you?

Determine, with your healthcare provider, how your organs are functioning. You can do that through diagnostic testing, like lab tests or saliva tests. In traditional Chinese medicine, we use pulse diagnosis. All these tests can help you identify if your organs are strong or weak. If you are strong, then you can do high-intensity interval trainings. You still can't do them seven days a week, but you can do more of them. If your organs are weak, you can do low-intensity exercises to prevent yourself from getting hurt. Ask yourself if what you are doing now is helping you or hurting you.

To summarize: Fitness is not as simple as people think, but it is also not as complex as people make it out to be. Only you can determine what the purpose of fitness is for you.

Is it to strengthen your organs, to regain health independence, and obtain optimal health?

Or are you a bodybuilder?

You need to figure out the true purpose. Once you know the purpose, you then need to identify the condition of your organs.

What can your body tolerate right now?

What will be beneficial, and what will be harmful?

Often, we need extra help. You need to find someone who understands this concept and can test your organs and help you identify the right type of fitness program for you.

In the previous section, we identified that there are different intensity levels in fitness.

We can also break them down into two categories:

1. Aerobic fitness
2. Anaerobic fitness

AEROBIC FITNESS

What comes to mind when you hear the term *aerobic fitness*?

Aerobic fitness is also known as *cardio*. It is exercise that strengthens your heart.

When you think about the term cardio, what comes to mind?

Great aerobic fitness includes activities such as:

- Walking
- Running
- Cycling
- Treadmill

- Elliptical
- Swimming

Should You Do Aerobic Fitness?

Should you be doing aerobic fitness?

That is the question.

Earlier, we talked about determining your goal. We also know that fitness is one of the five pillars of health.

And we discussed that you need to help two types of muscles: the heart and the muscles that hold up your spine. The heart is the most important muscle in the body. It is the only pump in your body. If there is one type of exercise you need to do, it is exercise that strengthens your heart. The heart is just a muscle, so it needs to be worked.

That is where aerobic fitness comes in. If you have a strong heart, you are pumping adequate oxygen to every single cell in your body. If you don't have a strong heart, your organs are going to be nutrient-deficient. It does not matter if you eat organic food and take all the supplements and vitamins you can find. If your heart is not pumping efficiently, then the nutrients you put in your mouth will not be able to be distributed to the right organs.

How do you determine if your heart is pumping efficiently?

There are diagnostics for that. You can go to your Western medicine doctor and do tests, or in Chinese medicine, we do functional pulse diagnosis which can help identify how the blood is circulating to your heart and how efficiently your heart is pumping. Because the heart is so important, everybody needs to take care of theirs.

Can You Walk Your Way to Optimal Health?

Aerobic fitness is so important, but can you just rely upon aerobic fitness to obtain optimal health?

No, you can't. In the previous section, I explained that there are two main muscles you need to focus on when it comes to fitness. One is your heart, and it is the most important muscle. The other area that you need to focus on is the group of muscles in your spine that hold your organs together.

Patients often tell us that they are walking a lot, so why is their health still in the dumps?

Why is my diabetes not reversing?

Why is my thyroid still low?

Why is my energy still low?

Why am I not sleeping?

They are helping their hearts, but that is not the only muscle you need to strengthen. You need to strengthen your other muscles, as well.

How much aerobic fitness you should do also varies. It goes back to how your organs are functioning.

How is your heart functioning?

If your heart is pumping weakly and inefficiently, you shouldn't be running or signing up for a marathon. You will just make it worse. On a side note, marathon runners may look like they are healthy, but they usually die early of heart disease because they overwork their hearts. In fact, marathon runners increase their cardiac risk by seven-fold. Researchers found that during a marathon more than half of the segments in your heart lose function due to an increase in inflammation and a decrease in blood flow, and this temporary heart damage may play a role in marathon deaths.[4]

If you do too much aerobic fitness, you will overwork your heart. The same is true with the rest of your body. If you overwork any organ in your body, it will eventually shut down. Yes, you can overwork your heart, so it's important to understand that you need

---

4   fitness.mercola.com/sites/fitness/archive/2012/05/11/peak-fitness-vs-running-marathons.aspx

to exercise at the right intensity. You must determine how the condition of your heart is at that time.

My father-in-law had quite a variety of cardiovascular issues. He had run a successful business, but then he lost everything. At the time, in order to sustain his successful business, he neglected his health. He had cardiovascular disease, hypertension, and diabetes. He moved in with my wife and me, and I educated him about fitness. He started power walking every day. Just from the power walking, he improved his heart function, so he no longer has hypertension, and his blood sugar has significantly improved.

He is a good example of how aerobic fitness can improve health, but by itself, it cannot get you to optimal health. Even though his blood pressure is normal, he still has diabetes. Aerobic fitness helped in one aspect, but it did not reverse another aspect. It still helped his blood sugar, don't get me wrong, and he's now prediabetic, but it is still not optimal. To reverse his diabetes completely, he needs to change his diet, which he is still working on.

Frequently Asked Questions

I'm approached by people who have never been fond of weight training, but they know they need to exercise. Their muscles are soft and out of shape, so they wonder if they can develop a nice body just by doing aerobic fitness.

The answer is no, you can't.

You need to understand that aerobic fitness focuses on your heart. If you want to change the shape of your body, you need to do resistance training, or *anaerobic* fitness, which we will talk about later. Often you can see this when you go to the gym: people spending countless hours on a treadmill or stationary bike but doing no resistance training. Observe them. You will see that their bodies never change; they don't develop muscle tone.

For people who want to lose weight: you may have been told that aerobic fitness burns more fat. If this is true, then everybody who is laboring on a treadmill should be losing weight like crazy. It doesn't happen. I'm not saying you don't need aerobic fitness, and I'm not saying it won't help, but it's not the main type of exercise necessary for weight loss. If you want to lose weight and chisel your body, aerobic fitness is necessary, but it's not the main focus.

Another issue I witness is that people constantly say they don't have time for aerobic fitness. You only need ten to thirty minutes, two to three times a week. It does not require a lot of time if you are doing the right exercise at the right time. Even if you travel and spend time in hotels, you don't need a treadmill. Power walk around the block. Run up stairs. There are so many ways to do aerobic fitness without a gym. The beauty of aerobic fitness is that you don't need anything except yourself, moving. That's it.

Aerobic fitness is crucial. Everybody needs to do aerobic exercise. The main reason is that aerobic exercise works the heart, which is the most important muscle in your body. Without the heart, you cannot survive. If blood circulation is an issue, if you have peripheral vascular disease or neuropathy, which are both circulation issues, it all starts from the heart.

When people take medications, like beta blockers or calcium channel blockers that decrease the force of the contractions of the heart, they may be helping their arrhythmia or their blood pressure, but these medications' purpose is to slow down the heart.

Disclaimer: I am not saying stop taking these medications; you need to consult with your physician about all medications.

If you slow down your heart, you will make everything worse. No wonder you feel so fatigued. No wonder your organs start malfunctioning. No wonder your neuropathy gets worse. You have shut down the only pump in your body. This is why aerobic fitness is so important.

ANAEROBIC FITNESS

Anaerobic fitness is also known as *resistance training*, which is about strengthening the muscles that hold your spine, bones, and organs in place. I don't know about you, but I don't want things jiggling around when they should not be. You want strong muscles to hold things in place.

For any of you who have had prolapsed organs or a prolapsed uterus, you understand that organs can slip. When I was interning at a clinic, there was a patient who had a prolapsed uterus; it was coming out of her cervix. These are weak muscles. In physical therapy, she did *Kegel exercises* — a specialty for toning the muscles of the pelvic girdle. This type of physical therapy exercise is anaerobic fitness because it is strengthening. To keep our organs in place, we need to strengthen our muscles.

What Is Anaerobic Fitness?

Anaerobic fitness is resistance training. It is putting stress on your muscles and on your bones in an effort to strengthen them. When you put stress on the muscles, you are making micro-tears in the muscles, which cause them to regenerate. As they regenerate, they get bigger. That is why people who lift weights say their muscles get bigger and bigger. You may not want to have big muscles and be a bodybuilder, but you still need strong muscles to function. The benefits of anaerobic fitness could be the solution to reversing osteoporosis.

Anaerobic fitness is the key to helping you lose weight and changing the shape of your body, simply through the process of breaking down and rebuilding your muscles. It's something aerobic training will not help you with. Too much aerobic training can hinder your progress, in fact, causing you to lose muscle mass and causing a slower metabolism.

It is anaerobic fitness that will help boost your metabolism.

What's All the Hype About Interval Training?

Interval training has become popular, especially programs like Insanity, P90X, and CrossFit. An example of interval training is walking on a treadmill at level three or four, speeding up to ten or eleven and, after a minute or so, dropping it back down to three or four again.

Interval training is the craze right now. It prevents your muscles from adapting to the same exercises done over and over. It speeds up the muscle-building process, and it is fairly effective. If you are not happy with the shape of your body and want to change it, interval training is the way to go. But be careful; as I mentioned, you need to make sure that your body can actually tolerate interval training, as not everybody can do it. You must make sure that it is the right type of exercise for you before you start doing it.

Also, interval training will help you burn fat faster than cardio training. If you want to burn fat, you need to implement interval training. It requires only ten to thirty minutes, two to three times a week, two hours per week, max. You don't need to be in the gym or doing CrossFit for an hour every day, and risk hurting yourself. It's just ten to thirty minutes each time.

Push-and-Pull Program

Clients who come to our training center can take classes on how they can regain control of their health by themselves. One class is a fitness class, which we call the *Push-and-Pull Program.*

Push refers to things like:

- Chest presses
- Bench flies
- Seated dumbbells
- Close-grip pushdowns for the triceps

Push means resistance-training exercises, in which you are pushing down or pushing forward. In the push program, you are working out your:

- Chest
- Shoulders
- Triceps

The *pull* program is the opposite. Pull exercises work out your:

- Back
- Biceps
- Abdominals
- Legs
- Quadriceps
- Hamstrings
- Calves

You only do two exercises for each muscle group. Each day that you are working out, you are only doing six types of exercises. That is why you can do it in thirty minutes. But you are working different muscle groups at each session.

First, perform warm-up sets, followed by sets performed to failure. The warm-up sets are one or two sets. If you are doing a flat bench fly, for example, then you may just put some weights on, but you are not straining, so do one set of eight to ten reps. That will be your warm-up.

Then you will do two sets to failure. *Set to failure* means that you lift weight until you cannot lift it anymore. I typically tell my patients to put on enough weight so their set to failure ends up being about twelve reps. If you end up doing fifty reps, there is too little weight on; you need more weight. That is what you will do for every single muscle group exercise.

Anaerobic exercise is the key component to:

- Fat burning
- Weight loss
- Reshaping your body

Anaerobic fitness may be the craze right now, but fitness crazes and trends change every year. Remember that anaerobic fitness is important, but it is not the only thing. You need to use it in conjunction with aerobic fitness if you want to obtain optimal health.

CHAPTER FOUR

Hormones and Organ Function

WHO DOES THE HEALING?

Hormones and organ function together make up one of the five pillars of health. Hormones are messengers between organs. Just like any relationship, you need proper communication, or there will be chaos. Each organ does not function by itself independently, irrespective of other organs. In fact, interconnection of the organs is the definition of holistic medicine: everything affects everything. If one organ malfunctions, it will affect others.

The way organs communicate is by secreting hormones. Hormones act as chemical messengers. The main control center for all these hormones is a part of the endocrine system, known as the *pituitary gland.* The pituitary gland, along with the hypothalamus, is the center for all hormone communication, and it regulates communication between all organs. We all need balanced hormones and functioning organs.

Does Your Doctor Heal You?

We are currently in a healthcare crisis. Our health system is currently set up for failure in regard to helping you regain your health independence. The current healthcare system is focused on making money for the pharmaceutical companies; it really has nothing to do with your health.

When do you go to your healthcare provider?

When you don't feel well.

When you go to that practitioner, what do you want them to do?

If you're like most people, you want your provider to tell you what is wrong with you, tell you what condition you have, and stick a label on you.

Why do you think that way?

You have been trained to think that way. If your doctor can give you a label or a diagnosis, then they are able to give you a medication, because pharmaceutical drugs are tied into diagnoses. Diagnoses are irrelevant; they only indicate what medication you are going to be given.

In these situations, does medication heal you, or does your doctor heal you?

Neither does. Most Western-trained health professionals are trained to prescribe you medication, which does not address the root cause of your problem and only masks your symptoms to give you the illusion that everything is well.

Who really does the healing in this situation?

If you haven't guessed yet—it's you.

Nobody can do the healing for you. Only you. You are in charge of your own health.

You cannot expect doctors to do it, because they will not do it. They are going to prescribe you a medication, which will not reverse your health condition. It will mask and manage it. If you are looking for someone to heal you, you must look to yourself. Look at the person in the mirror because there is no one in this world who can heal you but yourself.

Guess Who Is Responsible for 95 Percent of Your Healing?

We have established that doctors can't heal you because they will only give you a medication or perform some surgery to alleviate your symptoms. Healing is restoring your God-given function. The majority of us were born with all functioning organs. Something happened between the time when we were born, typically with 100 percent function, and now, when we may have only 50 percent function.

What happened?

The cause is you.

What did you do during this time?

What lifestyle changes did you make?

What dietary changes did you make?

It's what you did that caused the decreased functionality. If you took excess medications, you are the one responsible. No one can force you to eat something you don't want to eat, no one can force you to exercise, no one can force you to do anything you don't want to do. You are in control of your own body.

If you can't come to that realization, then you are never going to heal. You need to look to yourself to heal, because it's your own body that does the healing.

You were born with the given ability to heal, but you must do two things:

1. Remove what is interfering.
2. Supply what is missing.

It is all up to you. Doctors and other healthcare practitioners can help guide you, but what we providers do only affects 5 percent of your health. It's what you do on a day-to-day basis that affects 95 percent of your health. I cannot emphasize it enough: what you do on a day-to-day basis determines your health.

Were You Born With Too Many Organs?

My wife's aunt was born with three kidneys, so there are situations where people are born with an extra organ. It is rare, but it does happen. Most us were not born with too many organs.

Let me ask you this: if you were not born with too many organs, and thus were born with all the organs that were needed to be functioning at 100 percent — and the majority of us were born that way — why would you consider taking an organ out when something is not working?

Do you think that removing an organ is not going to affect the rest of your body?

We were born with the right number of organs. If you take one out, that will affect the communication between other organs. The organ is gone; there is nothing to communicate with now.

That creates chaos in your body:

- More hormone imbalance
- More organ dysfunction
- Other organs need to pick up the slack

When your gallbladder is removed, for example, you will have digestion problems for the rest of your life. Physicians don't tell you this. When you remove your gallbladder, it creates extra work for your liver. Your liver is already overworked. It detoxes every single thing you put in your body. It has enough work to do.

Imagine you are at work and given several tasks, and then someone quits and you assume their responsibilities, too, when you are already overwhelmed. Taking on someone else's responsibilities means you are only going to be more overwhelmed.

Guess what will happen?

You will tire out, and that is exactly what happens to your organs. If your gallbladder is removed, then your liver will be overworked, and your liver will start to give out and malfunction. If it malfunctions and stops detoxifying everything you put in your mouth, then you will retain toxins.

You can see how this cascade of effects happens just by removing an organ. I'm not saying organs shouldn't be removed, because there are situations when that may be necessary. The general consensus is you don't remove an organ if you don't need to.

This whole section is about who does the healing. We have established that you do the healing. Nobody else does the healing for you. You need all the organs in your body to do the healing. If you take one out, you will lose the ability to heal yourself.

If you are relying upon someone else, like your doctor or insurance company, to keep you healthy, then you are going to be heading toward the grave quickly. You will accelerate your aging process. The best way to heal your body is for you to look at yourself and examine what you are doing. What you do on a daily basis affects 95 percent of your health. What anybody else can do can only affect your health 5 percent. Your health is in your hands. Until you decide to make the decision to take control of your health, nothing is going to change.

ARE YOUR ORGANS COMMUNICATING?

I briefly touched on this previously, but organ communication is so crucial. As in any sort of relationship, communication is vital. Just try going home and not talking to your spouse for a week, and see what happens. Don't talk to your best friends at school, and see what their reactions are. It's usually not good.

If your organs did the same thing, what would happen?

You can see how communication among organs is so important. The lack of proper communication causes problems. That is how organs start to malfunction, and that is why you start feeling symptoms.

Symptoms of poor communication among your organs include:

- Insomnia
- Fatigue
- Chronic pain
- Weight gain
- Blurred vision
- Poor memory
- Hair loss

These are not the cause; they are the result of poor communication.

Hormones Are the Messengers

The way that your organs communicate is through hormones, which are messages between organs. For example, your pituitary gland communicates with your thyroid gland by secreting a hormone called the *thyroid-stimulating hormone* or *TSH*. The most common thyroid hormone test that most physicians use tests for TSH. It's not a complete representation of your thyroid function, but it's the gold standard for thyroid testing.

We need to make sure that each hormone is communicating effectively. To do that, we need to look at the hormones and understand why they are so important. Many people are familiar with hormones related to sexual development, but there's more to it than sex hormones. Insulin is a hormone. So are cortisol and adrenaline. The beauty of today's Western medicine technology is that we can measure all these hormones. These hormones can tell us if your organs are communicating, if they are not, or if they are sending the wrong messages. Even in marriages, sometimes the husband says something, and the wife interprets it as a different message.

How do we know if the organs are communicating?

We can see the response of the organ. Let's say the pituitary gland communicates with the thyroid gland by secreting TSH. The pituitary gland is telling the thyroid gland to produce thyroid hormones. We can measure that. If the thyroid gland does not produce thyroid hormones after the TSH was secreted, we know the thyroid gland either did not receive the message or misinterpreted the message. These are things that we can test, and these are things we need to look for when we are looking at organ communication.

Our Multitasking Organs

Our organs have many functions, more than what can be found in the anatomy and physiology textbooks in medical school.

For example, the liver:

- Detoxifies the body
- Helps regulate cholesterol
- Helps produce bile to aid digestion.

What Western medicine does not recognize is that the liver also helps regulate our emotions and our moods, including:

- Anxiety
- Depression
- Stress
- Irritability

It also helps regulate a woman's menstrual cycle. If you are having problems with your menstrual cycle, it may have to do with your liver function. The liver also controls the healing and production of your nails, tendons, and ligaments. If you get tendonitis a lot or your ligaments tear easily, that is because of a liver dysfunction.

The liver also controls your eyesight. Liver function will dictate how good your vision is. These functions of the liver were all discovered three thousand years ago in Chinese medicine. However, Western medicine is slowly catching up and learning about these functions of our organs.

The liver is just an example. All our organs have multiple functions that today's science has not discovered yet, but which have been around for three thousand years. Science is proving this, one by one.

The gut is another example. Science has finally discovered that the gut is our second brain. Chinese medicine knew this before, but recently Western medicine found out that *serotonin,* which is a neurotransmitter in the brain, is mostly produced in the gut, not in the brain.

That is why the gut affects mood. And why we talk about knowing something as a *gut feeling*. I think that's where it comes from, but it makes perfect sense. The gut produces serotonin, and serotonin makes you feel good. This is just another example of how our organs have so many more functions that Western medicine still does not know about.

Are Your Hormones Resisting Balance?

Just as we want to be sure our organs follow the commands that they are given, we want to be sure our hormones are in balance. I used the pituitary and thyroid gland example earlier: if the thyroid gland does not produce the thyroid hormone after being told to do so by the pituitary gland, then it is not following instructions. It is resisting the balance; the pituitary gland is sending the message to maintain balance, but the message is not being received.

Why would the thyroid gland resist balance?

The thyroid gland could have a virus buried inside it, like mono or Epstein-Barr virus (EBV). If the EBV makes a home in the thyroid gland, it will cause the thyroid gland to ignore commands from the pituitary gland. It will cause the thyroid gland to react in the opposite way than it should.

Any hormone can be resistant to balance. A lot of us know about type 2 diabetes, which is insulin resistance. This is mostly self-induced, because it is what we eat or inactivity that causes insulin resistance. The resistance means that your hormones are not working. Your body is trying to communicate. The pancreas is creating insulin, and the insulin tells all the cells to take out sugar from the blood and put it into your cells, but the cells are not getting the message, or they are getting the message but ignoring it, or they cannot identify it.

Why would they do that?

Perhaps the cell walls' receptors are inflamed. The inflammation is deterring them; it is like a haze in front of their eyes so they cannot see or interpret the message. Therefore, they can't take the appropriate action.

These are just some examples of hormone resistance in your body.

Communication in our bodies, in our lives, and in our relationships is key. In fact, it is key to everything. Whether you are running a business or are in a job, if there is not proper communication, things don't happen according to plan, and things go haywire.

Your ability to find the root cause of your health problems and also know how to restore organ function depends on proper communication. You need to find any communication breakages in your body. If you can do that, you can find the root cause. If you can find the root cause, you can address it and fix the problem. After you fix your problem, your symptoms will go away.

HAVE YOU HAD THE PROPER TESTING?

In the previous section, we discussed the importance of communication, and I touched briefly upon how to identify if there was a communication break. Remember, communication is hormones, and hormones are organs communicating to each other.

Today's technology involves testing for these hormones. When we suspect there is a breakdown in communication, most likely there is a hormone imbalance. So, it is vitally important to properly test your hormone levels. It takes more than one simple test. We need to make sure we do the right test so we get a complete picture of what is going on in your body and in your health.

"My Labs Are Normal, but I Still Feel Like Crap."

Using the thyroid example, the gold standard of thyroid testing is for TSH, which is the communication between the pituitary gland and the thyroid gland. This does not give us the complete picture of what is going on with your thyroid hormones. You may have thyroid symptoms, but doing the TSH test does tell us if the problem is in your pituitary gland, your thyroid gland, or somewhere else.

Often, when you go to the doctor and test TSH levels, they automatically dive into the treatment.

What is the treatment if they suspect your thyroid hormones are low?

They give you a synthetic hormone, which can help bring your labs back to normal. When they see that your TSH level is back to normal, your doctor will tell you that the hormone is balanced and the job is done.

The problem is, you may still feel like crap, with symptoms such as:

- Fatigue
- Hair Loss
- Insomnia
- Dry Skin
- Vaginal Dryness
- Symptoms of thyroid disorder

But your labs are normal.

What does that mean?

Typically, what this means is you did not find the root cause. You used medication to manipulate your labs. Labs are important, but they can be manipulated with medication. When you manipulate them, that does not mean you solved the problem. To solve the problem, you must do the right testing. Until you do that, you may be stuck in this scenario, where your labs are normal but you still feel like crap.

Do You Have Yellow Caution Lights in Your Lab Ranges?

When you look at the results of your blood tests, you will see that the ranges are huge. Let me use testosterone as an example. One lab gives a normal range of 200 ng/dL to 800 ng/dL, which is a huge difference. If you are just above 200, at 201; or just under 800, at 799; your physician is going to tell you your testosterone is normal.

But how do you feel?

You will still feel like crap.

You need to understand what these ranges mean. They are based on sick people.

When was the last time you thought to yourself: *Hey, I feel great today, why don't I go to the lab to have my blood drawn so I can add my values to the blood test ranges?*

No one ever does that. If you are on either end of the low normal or high normal, you are heading toward a crisis situation.

In functional wellness, we slow down the process, putting yellow caution lights in your labs. Before you head toward these ends, you should already be doing something about it. You should be move toward figuring out how to reverse it. As you are going toward either extreme, things are starting to malfunction. You need to identify what is going on before it gets out of hand, or worse, becomes irreversible.

Let's say you had a child, and you were playing with him on your front lawn. Your kid saw his friend across a really busy street.

Would you watch your kid run out there and wait until he is about to step in the street and get hit by a car before you say anything?

No, you would tell your kid to slow down and look both ways for cars before he even reached that street. You put the yellow caution light in his path.

When you look at labs, you need to have those caution lights. If you are already heading toward either extreme of the ranges, you need to look at what is starting to malfunction. The sooner you identify it, the sooner you can reverse the problem and stop it from becoming a crisis situation. If it gets to be a crisis situation, you may get to a point where you can no longer reverse it. Labs are important, but you must know how to read them.

Testing to Get a Complete Picture

Let's go back to the thyroid example. The gold standard is the TSH test. Some physicians may do T4 or T3. However, those do not give you the whole picture. If you want to use labs, we have labs in Western medicine that give us the complete picture.

Why do physicians not use those?

It is because they do not have a solution, even if they find the problem. You need to measure your free T3, because free T3 is made by converting free T4 to free T3. Sixty percent of that conversion occurs in your liver.

Let's say the tests show your TSH is normal, but your free T3 is low. If you hadn't measured the free T3, you wouldn't have known there was a conversion problem. If there is a conversion problem, then the problem is not in your thyroid gland, but it is actually in the liver. To address the thyroid problem, we need to fix your liver, not your thyroid gland. When doctors give you synthroid or levo—*levothyroxine sodium,* typically prescribed for hypothyroidism—which is just T4, that is not solving the problem. The synthroid does not help your liver function better. You need to supply what is missing to help your liver function better.

When you look at cholesterol, you also need to look at your blood sugar. If you just measure cholesterol, you have no idea what is causing the cholesterol to go up. You know the liver is producing it, but you don't know why the liver is overproducing it. You also need to measure your blood glucose, because most of the time, it is excess sugar that causes the liver to secrete more cholesterol.

The problem here is not your liver producing too much cholesterol—it's that you have too much sugar. Unless you solve the excess sugar problem, you will always have a cholesterol problem. It does not matter if you are prescribed a statin, which will lower your cholesterol. It is superficially making your labs look normal, but it is not helping restore your liver function.

The root cause is sugar. Unless you address the sugar intake, you will never lower your cholesterol by yourself. This is why we need to use labs and the proper testing to get the complete picture. Without proper testing, we will not get the complete picture. If you don't have a complete picture, then you won't be able to solve the problem.

To summarize: we discussed using labs, but interpreting them in a different, functional way, not the way traditional allopathic medicine interprets them. You will not get the correct results otherwise. You also need to make sure that you get the correct labs. If you don't get the correct labs, you also won't get the complete picture. You need to get the correct labs and interpret them in a functional way.

Do labs by themselves give a complete picture?

No, they don't. There is no one type of medicine or one single test that can give us a complete picture of overall health.

This is why, in our clinic, we combine Chinese medicine with Western medicine, using functional pulse diagnosis, which was discovered three thousand years ago before there were MRIs or labs tests. They found that different sections of the radial pulse actually corresponded to different organs in the body. The radial artery has blood pumping through it, so, using functional pulse diagnosis, we can feel the blood flow going to all the organs in your body. This gives us another clue as to how your organs are functioning. We combine that with the lab diagnostics, and we get a more complete picture.

The more complete picture you have, the higher the chance you will find the specific root cause. If you can find the root cause, you can then address it, improve it, reverse it, and eliminate it. That will eliminate your symptoms. If you can do all these, then you can successfully heal yourself.

CHAPTER FIVE

Nervous System

WHO IS THE MASTER OF YOUR BODY?

When patients come to our office, they are wondering:

- *What have I done wrong?*
- *How did I get like this?*
- *What should I have done differently?*
- *Is there something I can do to get me out of this mess?*

The fact is, we do a lot of things right, but we also do some things that are not so beneficial for our health. To address that, we first need to look at the master control.

Who is the master of your body?

You need to know who is in control before you can do something about it. It's like finding the root cause; you must find out why things aren't working. If you don't find the root cause, then you are just chasing symptoms. If you just treat the symptoms by taking medication, you won't solve the problem. Then you will continue to do the wrong thing that is creating the symptoms. To determine the root cause, you need to understand who is the master of your body.

The Puppet Master

If you have ever been to a child's puppet show, you will know there is a master controller who is in charge of the puppet. We have a puppet master in our body, too. It's similar to your computer.

What is the master of the computer?

What makes everything work?

It's the *Central Processing Unit,* or CPU. Fortunately, we are prebuilt with a CPU, which is our brain, or more specifically, our *central nervous system.* The central nervous system includes our brain and spinal cord. All the nerves that come out of the spinal cord are called the *peripheral nervous system.*

But, when I am referring to the puppet master, I am referring to this CPU system, which controls everything. It dictates what goes on in your body:

- Your ability to heal
- Your ability to digest food
- Your ability to adapt to the outside environment

It is the master controller. Nothing happens without our puppet master sending out the command.

We need to look at the function of our puppet master. Is it in good health?

If it is not in good health, then everything else will be chaotic, too. We can look at brain health, for example.

How is your brain health?

Remember, in previous chapters, we briefly mentioned that your body has a second brain: the gut. But we will focus more on your first brain in this section.

The Puppet and the Strings

I consider the puppet to be your organs. The CPU has these wires that go to your organs, just like a puppet master is manipulating the puppet through the strings. Our central nervous system, or our puppet master, is controlling the puppets through its strings, which are the peripheral nerves. You can imagine physical nerves as physical wires that are connected from your brain and spinal cord to every single cell and organ in your body.

We've addressed the importance of good health for your brain. Your peripheral nerves dictate the communication between your puppet master and your puppets. If there is a problem with the strings, there will be a problem controlling the puppet. The same with your organs: if there is a disconnect in one of the nerves, that organ will not function correctly. It's like a frayed wire; there will be a short circuit.

To reestablish that connection, you need to find the root cause. You must decrease the inflammation of the nerve and restore the function of the nerve so your brain can send the right message to the right organ. If that occurs, and there is proper communication, then your organs will function perfectly.

The Creator

We know that the puppet master controls its puppet through its strings, and our CPU controls our organs through our peripheral nervous system.

How does it all function?

Why are we built with a functioning CPU?

I call that the Creator. It does not matter what religion you believe in, or if you believe in Darwinism, or if you believe we come from monkeys. Our bodies are a unique entity, a unique creation. We were built with an innate intelligence. That means we have an ability to heal and auto-regulate all our bodily functions.

Let me give you an example. When you are eating food, you don't need to think: *Okay, brain, digest the food.* It automatically happens. The same thing happens when you cut yourself with a knife and are bleeding.

You don't need to say: *Hey brain, let's stop this from bleeding.*

It just happens, because we are built with an innate intelligence.

Science cannot explain this, so far. The fact is we are born with this, and this intelligence allows your body to constantly adapt to an ever-changing environment. We have been given this innate intelligence to allow us to adapt to everything. That is a good thing and a bad thing.

If you are constantly taking medication, your body can adapt to the medication to the point where it becomes dependent upon it. That is a bad thing. But it can also adapt in the sense that if you get poisoned, you can still function. Our bodies have a built-in ability to quarantine the poisoned area so that the rest of the body can continue to function. Wherever you believe this innate intelligence came from, it resides everywhere in your body.

Because your brain and the rest of your nervous system mediate your innate intelligence, it stands to reason that this system should be optimized to its highest potential if you want optimal health to be achieved. We established that your CPU is your master computer, or your puppet master, and it regulates every function of your body for every second of your life. When it is out of sync, you are out of sync.

This is so important. We must consider the brain, spinal cord, and nervous system when we look at diseases. Remember, your body was built with innate intelligence to heal itself. If it is not healing itself, something is wrong, and we need to look for the cause. We need to look at the nervous system, your puppet master.

IS THERE SOMETHING WRONG WITH YOUR CIRCUITRY?

We have established that we need to look at the nervous system and see if it is functioning at its optimal level; if it's not, you are going to have problems.

What causes the master of your body to malfunction?

Often, it is something that is affecting your circuitry. If we can solve this, then we can get the master of your body to function up to par and be in balance so that you're back in balance. That is what we are going to address in these next few sections.

When we talk about things that affect your nervous system, we are talking about stress. Remember, there are three types of stress:

1. Physical
2. Chemical
3. Emotional

Physical Stress on the Master

The first is physical stress. Physical stress includes traumas, accidents, and sports injuries that you suffered a long time ago, as well as broken bones, over-exercising, and overdoing, running in marathons or triathlons. These are physical stresses on your body.

The opposite condition—such as the sedentary lifestyle of a couch potato—also creates physical stress because our bodies were made to move. If you don't move, you are creating physical stress because you are gaining weight, which is putting more stress on your bones and your heart. Your body then creates more veins and arteries to adapt to the excess weight you have gained, and your heart will be enlarged because it is not used to working so hard. All that places stress on your nervous system and your body.

If you are doing any of these consistently, then you must begin making adjustments to your lifestyle to reduce physical stress. That is how you address physical stress on the master.

Chemical Stress on the Master

The second type of stress is chemical stress.

What is chemical stress?

Medications are chemicals; they create chemical stress on your nervous system and your body.

Do you think that's good?

No.

When was the last time you heard of someone who was born with an Advil deficiency?

You haven't.

That is because medications do not belong in your body. They are chemically stressing to your nervous system and your brain.

What about the air you breathe, the water you drink, the food you eat?

All this creates chemical stress on your body. If you are putting junk food into your body, you will get junk in your blood. Unless you like to have junk in your blood, don't do it. Most of us who want to restore our health need to make sure we are putting the right fuel in our body and not creating chemical stress. This is why diet is so important.

My dad used to tell me *you are what you eat,* and that is so true. What you eat dictates your health. We have addressed diet in the past chapters, but this is just a reminder that the wrong type of diet can create chemical stress in your body. Be careful of fad diets, as they change from year to year. As I am writing this book, the current popular diet is the Paleo diet, which is not suitable for every person and not for long-term use, as it can create inflammation and chemical stress on the body.

Emotional Stress on the Master

When we talk about stress, usually the first thing people think about is emotional stress. Yes, emotional stress has a huge impact on your master. It is one of the main causes of all chronic degenerative diseases.

When you get stressed, this is what happens:

1. Your brain perceives an environmental danger.

2. It activates a part of your brain called the *amygdala,* which immediately fires a nerve impulse to the hypothalamus. That kicks off your fight-or-flight response, or your *sympathetic response.*

3. This stress response starts with the hypothalamus stimulating your pituitary gland, which

is your master hormone gland, to release a hormone called *adrenocorticotropic hormone,* or ATCH, which stimulates your adrenal glands to release cortisol, a stress hormone that, incidentally, makes you fat.

4. This cortisol causes a cascade of physical effects and functions designed to aid in your physical survival of the danger.

The bottom line is this: emotional stress causes your brain to constrict blood vessels, which affects blood circulation to different parts of your body. If you are constantly in a fight-or-flight mode, you won't be digesting. When you are running away from a dog that wants to bite you, your body will not be digesting food right then. It will be guiding blood to your muscles, heart, and lungs so you can run faster. If it guided blood to your stomach or digestive tract, you would get bitten in the butt instead of being able to run away.

If your body is in that constant fight-or-flight mode, you will have:

- Digestion problems (constipation, diarrhea)
- Absorption problems
- Energy problems
- Thyroid problems

This is why you must address the emotional stress. You may not be able to eliminate what is causing the stress, but you can help the organs—the ones that help you adapt to stress—function better.

When we look at finding the root cause of your master malfunctioning, we need to look at the three types of stresses. If we can find out which one is actually causing disruption in your nervous system, we can solve it. It is rarely just one of the three; usually, you have two or maybe all three, but one is usually more pronounced than the others. So, we need to find the cause of the stress. If we can eliminate that, your brain will function better.

If your brain functions better, it will be able to control the puppet-to-organ function, and once your organs are functioning better, all the symptoms you are facing will go away.

HOW TO RECONNECT THE CIRCUITRY IN YOUR BODY

We've discussed the master and what prevents the master from functioning, which are the nervous system and the three stresses. Now, we are going to discuss how to reconnect the circuitry, how to get the communication back to normal.

It is the communication that was the problem in the beginning. We need to look at how we can get the brain and the CPU to have better communication with your organs. We need to do two things:

1. Remove what is interfering from the communication.
2. Supply what is missing, which usually are nutrients.

If you have a spouse and the two of you are arguing all the time, you need to find out what is interfering with proper communication and remove it. After that, you need to nourish the relationship again; that is what is missing. I'm going to teach you how to do the same thing between your brain and your organs.

Jumpstart the Puppet Master

Nowadays, everybody has a computer.

When you are working on something, and suddenly your computer freezes, you probably think: *Oh, crap, did I save everything?*

You hit all the buttons and nothing changes.

What is the next step that you usually take?

You will hit the power button to restart the computer, because that is the only way you can get it to work again. Sometimes your body needs the same thing. It needs a jumpstart; it needs the reset button.

You need to reset your puppet master, your CPU. It's like using a defibrillator on someone whose heart just stopped beating. All you're doing is resetting the circuitry in the body.

One of the best tools to reset your circuitry and jumpstart your puppet master is acupuncture, which has been used for three thousand years to reconnect the communication between your brain and every organ in your body. It can reestablish those disconnects, those frayed wires. The same way you reset your computer, an acupuncture needle stimulating your nervous system can reset your nervous system and stimulate your brain to communicate with the correct organ again.

Free Up the Puppet Master

We discussed that acupuncture is one of the best tools, and I would say probably the only natural tool, to jumpstart and reset your nervous system.

What if something is actually pushing on your nerves?

What if the interference is something that was pushing on your circuitry?

If a bone is pushing on your circuitry, you need to readjust the bone so it is not pushing on your nerves. If it did, it would affect everything.

If you have a hose that you are using to water your garden, and someone steps on your hose, does that increase or decrease the water output?

It decreases it. The same is true with your nerves. If something is pushing on your nerves, it will decrease the message, so you need to remove anything pushing on the nerves.

One of the best tools for that is chiropractic. Chiropractic is good in removing the physical bone that is pushing on your nerves, which acupuncture cannot do. Chiropractic is beneficial, and it should be included in your treatment plan to regain your health.

However, chiropractic cannot reset your nervous system like acupuncture can. The best approach is to have both acupuncture and chiropractic at the same time. One can reset your nervous system, and the other can remove any physical interference that is pushing on the nerves. The combination will give you phenomenal results.

Make the Puppet Master Dance

In the previous two sections, we discussed two medical services that can assist you in reconnecting the circuitry in your body and getting your nervous system to function better. But you are probably wondering what you can do at home.

Do I have to rely on someone to do acupuncture and chiropractic on me?

What can I do at home to free up the circuitry?

There are some things you can do.

One thing we teach in our office as part of our wellness-training program is something called *acupressure*. Our acupressure is different than what you can find on Google searches. Our acupressure does not use our hands to push on the acupuncture points.

We actually give you a tool called a *Piezo pen* that mimics the stimulation of acupuncture needles. We give our patients a comprehensive map of the nervous system, which includes all the acupuncture points. We teach our patients how to apply the pen to a specific nerve which can elicit a specific response. For example, if someone has right shoulder pain, we tell them to stimulate their left calf with the tool. Ninety percent of the time, that will instantly decrease the shoulder pain.

If you have the right information, you can maintain your nervous system by yourself. If you get into an accident, that is a whole different story. If you have minimal-to-no structural issues in your body and your spine, then this acupressure program can be effective in helping you maintain your own nervous system and spinal health by yourself at home.

We have discussed the three main tools that you can use to reconnect the circuitry in your body:

- Acupuncture
- Chiropractic
- Our QRA (quick relief acupressure) program

It is important that you use these, because I have not found any other tool or service that can reconnect the circuitry. If you are serious about regaining control of your own health, then you need to take care of the master, which is your brain. You must take care of it. If you don't take care of it, then everything else crumbles.

I encourage you to invest in your health. Find a skilled acupuncturist or chiropractor so they can get the process started and help you gain some momentum, because we all need that. Being an acupuncturist myself, I understand that, because I do acupuncture on myself and my family. Obviously, if you don't have that skill, you need to find someone who does and can help you jump-start things. Otherwise, you could do it by yourself.

But let me ask you this: Do you want to take twenty years to get healthy, or do you want to take just one year?

I'm not saying it will take one year, but I am addressing the difference of time. Most of us don't have that much patience. If you want to improve your health quickly, acupuncture and chiropractic are two things you definitely need to do. You cannot do without them if you want optimal health.

Conclusion

Hopefully I have fulfilled my promise by providing you with a brief education, information, and insight into your health and what you need to do to take control of it so that you can enjoy health independence for the rest of your life.

This book was meant as a road map to guide you in the right direction; a starting point, so to speak. Finding solutions is the tricky part. The whole process hopefully has been simplified enough to let you know where to start, because sometimes taking that first step is the most difficult.

I want to help you make that first step. This book was designed to give you some background and debunk any misinformation, so you can ask the right questions and understand what is going on in your body.

I highly encourage you to read this book multiple times. I promise you will pick up new nuggets and gems every time you read it. I know from my own experience that with every book I've read five or six times, I pick up something new. Take notes. Hopefully you already did.

You now have the right information so you can seek the right help; it has been my goal to teach you where and from whom to seek help. The shortest distance between two points is a straight line, and I hope I provided that straight line, so you know whom to talk to and whom to seek help from. This may not be your current physician or healthcare practitioner; you may need to find someone else.

I encourage you to take control of your own health, because no one can change your health for you.

Who does the healing?

It's you.

Your doctor can't heal you. Ninety-five percent of wellness is self-care. So, you must start taking responsibility of your own health.

Zig Ziglar, America's most influential and beloved encourager, said to a crowd, "Think of three things that could really positively affect your health. At the same time, I also want you to think of three things you could do right now that could negatively impact your health."

He then asked what the commonality was between these two exercises. Both of them are your choice. It's up to you to make that choice, not someone else. It's up to you. Take action. Make the changes. If being healthy were so easy, everyone would be healthy. You may have heard that before.

If you want more information or need more assistance, my training center is here to help. You can visit our website at AchieveIntegrativeHealth.com. Our clinic strives to educate and empower you to make educated decisions about the health of your family members and yourself.

I don't know if you have ever had a mentor or coach to train or guide you in regaining your health. I wholeheartedly believe in mentors. I have a mentor for every aspect of my life, because I want the shortcut. I don't want to spend twenty years learning what my mentor spent twenty years learning. I don't want to spend the hundreds of thousands of dollars that they spent to get this information. That is the reason I hire coaches: I want that information now instead of waiting twenty or thirty years.

If you would like a mentor or coach, or if you don't know and want to figure it out, come join us at one of our free trainings. It will be an amazing experience!

Next Steps

To learn more about upcoming Health Training books, like us on Facebook: facebook.com/achieveintegrativehealth.

To learn more about the services offered by our clinic and training center, visit us at: achieveintegrativehealth.com.

About the Author

Jimmy Yen is a licensed acupuncturist, herbalist, anti-aging and wellness expert, public speaker, and a specialist in natural solutions to restore health. He has been featured by Fox News, CBS-Keye Austin, AOMA graduate school for Integrative Medicine, TNA Facial Pain Association, Sjogren's Syndrome Foundation, Rotary International, Texas Association of Acupuncture and Oriental Medicine, Texas A&M University, Natural Grocer's, and Community Impact. He is a member of the medical advisory committee for the Neuropathy Alliance of Texas (a Texas chapter of the Neuropathy Association).

Jimmy began his training at the University of Texas at Austin, where he studied Biochemistry prior to completing his training in traditional Chinese medicine, acupuncture, herbal medicine, and nutrition. Jimmy is the founder and CEO of the ACHIEVE Integrative Health Center in Austin, Texas, where he practices Functional Wellness, mentors and trains physician assistants, physicians, chiropractors, and acupuncturists about his specific systems and solutions. His purpose and mission is to educate, train, and develop Wellness Warriors in his community about how to regain control of their health naturally, without drugs and surgery, and gain health independence for the rest of their lives.

www.ingramcontent.com/pod-product-compliance
Lightning Source LLC
Chambersburg PA
CBHW052131300426
44116CB00010B/1862